LIAM AND OLIVIA GO TO LAS VEGAS

Written and illustrated by Julie Given

Willow Tree Books
Beamsville, Ontario

Published by Willow Tree Books
Beamsville, Ontario, Canada

Printed by KDP
ISBN 979-8-280-93019-3

This is a work of fiction. Any resemblance to actual persons, living or dead, or actual events is purely coincidental.

WILLOW TREE
BOOKS

For Shane

Liam and Olivia stepped into the sunshine, eyes wide at the giant signs and palm trees.

"This place looks wild already!" Olivia said. "Let's see what adventures Las Vegas has for us!"

Their first stop was the famous "Welcome to Las Vegas, Nevada" sign.

They posed with big smiles as the sun beamed behind them. "We're officially in Las Vegas!" Liam cheered.

It was time to visit the famous water fountains at the Bellagio hotel!

Water shot high into the sky, dancing to the music and Liam and Olivia watched as the fountains sparkled in the sunlight.

"It's like the water is putting on a show for us!"

It was time to visit the Pinball Hall of Fame.

Liam and Olivia ran from machine to machine, pulling levers and hitting buttons. "This one has a wizard!" said Liam.

"Mine has a space alien!" Olivia laughed as bells rang and lights flashed.

At the Flamingo Hotel, real pink flamingos waded in a garden pond.

"They're so fancy and fluffy!" Olivia said.

Liam pointed, "That one looks like it's doing ballet."

Liam and Olivia visited Circus Circus!

Inside the Adventuredome, they rode bumper cars, played carnival games, and screamed with joy on a mini roller coaster.

"This place is like a giant indoor fair!" Liam shouted.

Next, they visited the Downtown Container Park.

They climbed a giant playground and slid down twisting tubes.

"Let's do that one again!" Olivia said, racing Liam back to the top.

They passed a tiny white chapel with twinkly lights.

A couple stepped outside in wedding clothes. Liam and Olivia waved.

"I think they just got married!" Olivia whispered with a smile.

Liam and Olivia found four floors of chocolate candy store fun!

They filled bags with colourful candy and took a photo with a giant red candy.

"Let's find the best flavour!" Liam said.

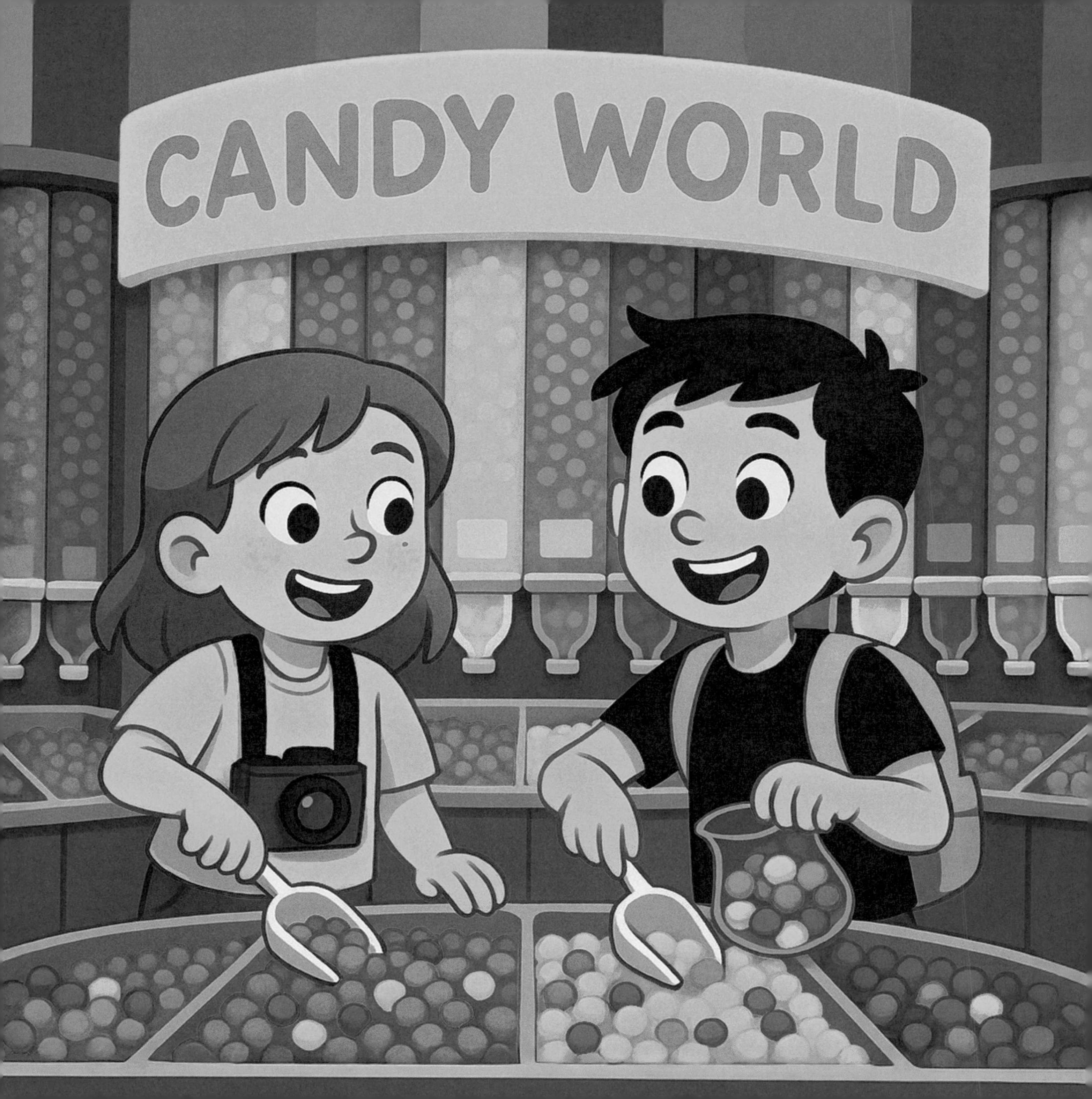
CANDY WORLD

They posed with a chocolate Statue of Liberty and tried a cookie bigger than their heads.

"This place smells like dessert!" Olivia said.

At Mandalay Bay, they walked through a glass tunnel surrounded by sharks, stingrays, and glowing fish.

"Look! That shark's smiling at us!" Liam said.

At the Ethel M. Chocolate Factory and Cactus Garden, they peeked through windows to watch chocolate being made, then wandered outside through rows of prickly plants.

"That cactus looks like it has arms!" Olivia laughed.

At the Discovery Children's Museum, they launched paper rockets, built bridges, and climbed a huge indoor tower.

"We could spend all day here!" Liam said, as he started another game.

They passed by the Mirage Volcano Show.

Boom! Fire shot into the air as music played and mist swirled around.

"It's like a real volcano erupting!" Liam said. "Except cooler—and safer!" Olivia added.

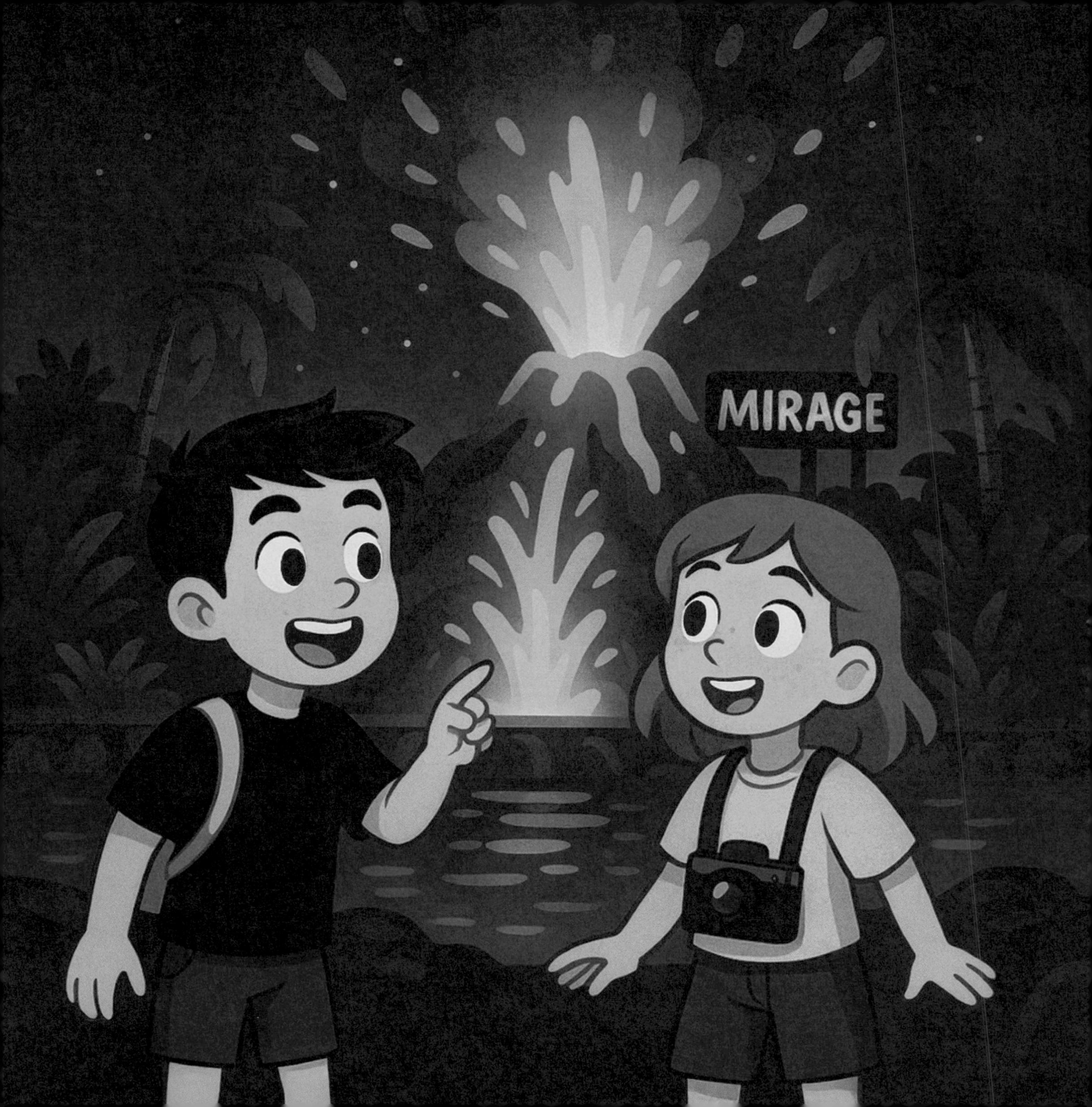
MIRAGE

They walked through lobbies with giant castles, glowing pyramids, and even a replica of New York City.

"Each one feels like its own little world," Liam said.

They watched a magician pull scarves from his sleeve and make a bunny disappear.

"How did he do that?!" Olivia gasped.

They found a colourful carousel inside a shopping mall.

Liam rode a giraffe.

Olivia picked a sparkly unicorn.

"Let's go again!" they both said.

They shared a huge sundae piled with candy, sprinkles, and whipped cream.

"Best. Snack. Ever." Liam said, with a chocolatey grin.

Liam and Olivia stepped into a giant glass pod on the High Roller.

As it rose, the city stretched out below them.

"We're taller than the buildings!" Liam said. Olivia pointed. "I see the fountains and the pink hotel!"

They grinned as Vegas sparkled all around them.

As the sky got dark, Liam and Olivia spotted a giant glowing ball in the distance.

The whole surface shimmered with stars and swirling galaxies

"It looks like outer space!" Olivia said.

Liam stared in awe. "It's like the moon landed right here in Las Vegas!"

Before bed, they took one last silly selfie with their souvenirs.

"We need a whole album just for this trip!" Liam laughed.

The next morning, they looked out the hotel window one last time.

"What happens in Vegas..." Olivia started.

"Goes in our memory book forever," Liam finished.

Also by this author:

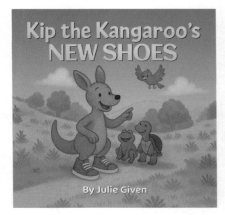

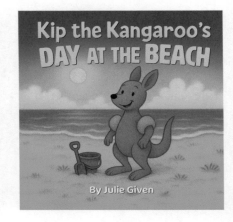

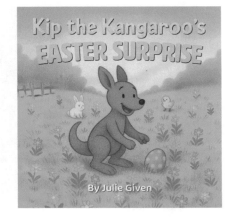

Made in the USA
Columbia, SC
12 June 2025

59354329R00029